Lacrimarium

Kayil York

Lacrimarium

Kayil York

Other books

Roses & Thorns
Bleeding Caverns
11:11
You Deserve More
Brave Soul
Heartwork Therapy

Lacrimarium

Kayil York

Lacrimarium
By Kayil York
Cover Art
By Mitch Green
Copyright © 2023

All Rights Reserved

License Notes
No part of this publication may be reproduced, distributed or transmitted in any form or by any means including photocopying, recording or other electronic or mechanical methods without the prior written permission of the author, except in the case of brief quotations embodied in critical reviews and certain other noncommercial uses permitted by copyright law.

Lacrimarium

Lacrimarium Playlist

"break my bones" – Matt Hansen
"Let Go" – Asking Alexandria
"Breath With Me ft. Lindsey Sterling" – Lacey Sturm
"Outrunning." – Ryan Jesse
"God's Eyes" – Dax
"Land of The Heroes" – Alan Walker, Sophie Stray
"Last Resort – Reimagined" – Falling in Reverse
"Rain" – Sleep Token
"Flying :))" – Tom Odell
"Wish You The Best" – Lewis Capaldi
"Baby Lacrimarium – VV
"LET EM PRAY" – NF
"Unfamiliar" – Currents
"Drowned in Emotion" – Caskets
"I'm Sorry" – Armin van Buuren, Scott Abbot
"Leave a Light On" – Papa Roach
"strangers" – Camylio
"Breathe" – Greg Maroney
"something to remember – Matt Hansen
"Below The Belt ft. Set It Off" – Point North, Set It Off
"Anymore" – Lø Spirit
"f.u.n!" – 44phantom
"Our Time Will Come" – Redl
"Like A Cigarette" – Besomorph, Saint Chaos
"cut my fingers off" – Ethan Bortnick
"better of without me" – Matt Hansen

Lacrimarium

Kayil York

I dedicate this book to my sisters.
The ones who have been with me through some of the hardest times of my life and have spoken nothing but life, healing, and wisdom into me.

Lacrimarium

Kayil York

Healing is so rough because we choose to open our hearts for love, only to endure the pain of their goodbye.

In this mourning, they will be enveloped in your tears. Carving their name in the caverns of your heart. Leaving you with the shape of a memory without the soul of what once filled it.

It is entirely up to us on healing those holes, sewing up our heart with the needed forgiveness so that we can find and apply peace to our lives.

Lacrimarium

Psalms 56:8 NLT
"You keep track of all my sorrows. You have collected all my tears in your bottle. You have recorded each one in your book. You've kept track of my every toss and turn through the sleepless nights, each tear entered in your ledger, each ache written in your book."

Lacrimarium

Kayil York

With all the pain they caused,
I have to heal and move on.
I barely made it out with what little
was left of me.

You have to forgive yourself for the times you gave too much away while they took advantage of you. You have to forgive yourself for making the kind of mistakes that broke your heart. Because you know better now. *You have to forgive yourself for the past.* You may not be able to forget it. But in forgiving yourself, you are implanting an abundance of peace into your soul which will allow you to move forward from what you thought you couldn't get passed.

Tears are the only thing you can control when it comes to your emotions. Because they hold *your* happiness, *your* pain, all of *your* emotions. They hold your senses of what makes you feel in the depths of your soul. Let them come and go as they need to.

Every piece of your life is a part of your story. Not every part was easy to bear or get through because it wasn't what you deserved. Life hands us so much pain in situations that don't seem to belong to us. But they happened for a reason. Even though it broke us into pieces, out bloomed some of the greatest blessings that gave us more purpose than we could have imagined. Every part of your story is there to give your life purpose, meaning, and a legacy that no one else can offer. So instead of dwelling on the hard parts you wished to forget, try to recognize what good came out of those situations. You are not you without the parts of yourself that came from the darkest depths into the brightest of lights.

With everything you are, keep your feet planted as you walk through life. There are many kinds of storms that will pull you off the path you're walking on. The rain will beat down on you. The road will fall away and you're met with a cliff you have to walk off in order to get back on track. You'll fall sometimes. Parts of your spirit will break. Your heart will feel defeated. But as long as you keep your mind strong, your soul steady, and your feet firmly planted, you will walk to the greatest places and leave your mark. Even when you fall off the path from time to time, don't be afraid to get back up, dust yourself off and keep going. There is a resilience inside of you that can't go out unless you let it. So, keep moving. Because you're not going anywhere you shouldn't be.

Lacrimarium

Forgiveness isn't necessarily
about the other person.
It's about healing your own heart
in order to restore peace inside your soul.

Kayil York

A word of advice— you're going to continue to get hurt when you expect too much from people who are too busy for you. Who say they care but don't actually show it. Who are so back and forth you never know what to think. Those people are not your people. And they certainly don't deserve anymore of your time or energy. You simply deserve better.

You hurt hard because you love hard. It's not because you want the hurt, but you want to show others that there is love in the world that can be big enough to meet you where you're at. Even if you're at your worst, you can still be loved with the best.

Kayil York

It's been too long, and now is the time to pick up your broken pieces so you can try to be whole again. I know the hurt is deep. I know the pain has been crippling. But you don't need to have it hold you back from the light that's trying to shine on you. Reach for it, hold the light. Let it spread through you so it can reach the places that ache. You've been living in darkness for far too long, my darling. It's time to heal those places and come back to yourself. Your pieces may be put back differently, but at least your courageous enough to become someone better than before. Someone you can come to love more because of the way you chose to come out of what you thought would destroy you.

Don't stop growing just because it hurts to confront your issues. Sure, it doesn't feel good to see your mistakes and the damage it caused to the people you love. But don't prevent yourself from learning how you can do better for next time because you don't like what you see. You're constantly going to be a work in progress and you can't get everything right. That is ok. Because choosing to work on yourself to become a better version may be a long road, but it's teaching you who you don't want to be anymore. Don't stop growing because it's hard. Let it push your boundaries beyond its limit so you can reach the version of yourself that's ready to meet you.

Kayil York

When you get out from under the abuse, walk at your own pace into healing. Because you don't just come out of a painful situation in a few days or even months. There is a layering to that kind of healing. It is discovering the new place you're in to see if it's safe. It's rediscovering who you are, finding the identity that they stripped you of. It's figuring out what you're new normal is, because what you left was far from it. Healing is trying to love yourself again after spending so much time hating yourself for what you accepted for so long. Even though you're in a new place it can still be painful. But moving in the right direction starts by making yourself safe. Any steps towards that is closer to the place you deserve to be at.

You don't need to validate who you are to people who don't want to understand you, who don't know you personally, and who do nothing but assume or project on you.
This is an important lesson so you don't lose yourself trying to get the approval of others who don't value you.

Kayil York

In hindsight, I realized that it was not ok for me to apologize after it was *you* that hurt *me*. I spent too much of my life apologizing for things that were not my fault. But I felt the need to remedy the situation because I didn't want the conflict. I figured if I took the fall for it all it would make everything better. Yet I was doing a disservice to myself by sweeping things under the rug, when what I really needed to do was fight for myself in speaking out about the way they hurt me.

Do not apologize for the space you take up in this world. If you're too much for someone, don't break yourself into pieces to try and fit in the way they prefer to see you.
Let your wholeness blind them.

Kayil York

It's ok to let people go, especially when they have been nothing but toxic to you. The hard part is not allowing them to make you feel guilty for making a decision that doesn't fit their agenda but increases your quality of life.

It takes time to accept yourself after spending most of your life not understanding who you were because it was dictated by others. It takes effort to develop your bravery in standing on your own after constantly giving into what everyone wanted. And it takes a great deal of healing your own heart and soul after years of giving everyone the power to constantly break it.

Kayil York

Sometimes you have to give up on people that shamelessly treat you like you're less than what you are. You don't need to keep giving and giving and giving to deplete yourself. There comes a point where you have to save yourself from the ones who do nothing but use you, abuse you, only to leave you. Its ok to quit on those people. You're meant to have genuine relationships with people who reciprocate the same energy. Don't settle. Because despite what they have made you believe, there are others out there who will treat you with the love and care you deserve.

It's going to hurt to heal those wounds, my darling. I know how difficult it has been to carry the weight around all these years. But I promise that once you start putting back the pieces, the healing will come. The peace will settle. The waves of pain will start to subside. It will take time, yes. But don't give up on yourself and the power you have to heal the places they broke.

She was stronger now because when rock bottom hit and the hardest punches were thrown, she still got back up. It took her a little while to feel any kind of bravery to get up off the floor. But once she did, she became someone she's never known. A lot less broken, a little more intense, and a lot more powerful in knowing what's she's capable of. That is the most powerful thing you can learn is how strong you can become when the brokenness has given you no choice but to rise.

I'm done apologizing for making the situation better when I haven't done anything wrong. I'm done being the scapegoat and taking the fall for everything in attempts to make the situation better. I'm not going to keep giving in to keep the peace. I'm going to stand up for myself and for my feelings. If it brings war, I'm ready to fight.

Kayil York

Don't lose *yourself* to keep *them*.
You are never meant to take away from yourself in order to gain the love from others. It's a long road back, a hard road back, and a difficult place to figure out who you are after giving so much away.
Don't *lose* yourself to *keep* them.
Who you are will attract the right people meant to be a part of your life who won't make you subtract from yourself to add to their personal gain.

You're going to intimidate people who are not on your level. It's not a matter of *if*, it's *when*. Don't allow their judgement to chip fragments of yourself away. You were not meant to be put in a box because others lack the potential you're capitalizing on. When you're chasing the dreams your heart is set on, sometimes you have to go it alone. That means getting up every day, doing what you do, and not allowing the critics to keep you from flying.

Kayil York

If you need to make yourself less accessible for the sake of your mental health, take all the time you need. Sometimes a step back is absolutely necessary in getting your head in the right place and your heart to be steady. You can't get yourself in the right place mentally if you don't take some space to sort out the mess. Take your space, take your time, and sort through your chaos. The storms always bring the rain, but the sun will shine its face again when the storm is ready to move on.

Lacrimarium

When you're unsure on how to move forward from a situation you're out of your element in, pray for wisdom and understanding. If that doesn't come, then pray to have the faith to get you through what you don't understand.

It's ok to share your feelings when someone has hurt you. That's how you resolve conflict; with healthy communication and understanding. When it turns into the other person twisting the reality of the situation to fit their egotistical narrative, that is not healthy. You shouldn't have to fight someone's ego in attempt to fix the relationship. If they truly value their relationship with you, they will put their ego aside so you can get to the root of the problem to fix it. Remember, it's *you* against the *problem*. Not *you* against *each other*.

Heal. So you're not bleeding all over people who didn't cause the pain.

Heal. So you can learn the value of moving forward in living a life of purpose and not destruction.

Heal. So that you don't become bitter in the situations that you really have no control over.

Heal. So you can discover the happiness of wholeness.

If they're fighting just to fight without trying to come to a resolve, just stop. Don't give them anymore of your energy. Don't waste another breath. You're sending your feelings, attempted resolutions, and reason onto deaf ears. When this is the case, you're better off closing your mouth and walking away. You can't get anywhere with people who are committed to keeping the issues fresh and against you. You're better off cutting ties and moving on from the dysfunction to keep yourself safe from their abusive behavior.

Life is so difficult and full of these crazy obstacles we are constantly getting through. Give yourself more credit for what you've had to do in order to make it. I know it's hard and most of the time you feel like you're defeated before the day even starts. Just listen, you are a strong and fierce soul. You have so much strength in you that you're not seeing. So let me tell you. Let me encourage you. Keep fighting through these days because you are never given more than you can handle. You've got this. You can do this. Even if no one else believes in you, know that I do.

Kayil York

Listen, the wound may not have been your fault. And you probably didn't deserve that pain either. But your healing is entirely your responsibility. No one has the power to heal the hurt in your soul but yourself.

There's always a price to pay when you establish your boundaries. Sometimes it comes with losing friends, sometimes it's family or a loved one. But the important thing to remember is not to lose yourself. As long as you keep you, it's ok to lose everyone else. Sometimes it's absolutely necessary in order to save who you are and who you're becoming.

Kayil York

You're going to miss the people you had to let go of. For a long time, it's going to hurt trying to heal that hole within your heart. But after a while, the wounds will close and the darkness will move so you can find the light within to heal what you fought through hell for.

Looking back, I recognized that for so long I would make myself small because I was afraid of being who I was. But I found out how to outgrow that fear and turn it into power. Because I was tired of feeling like I was never good enough to the people I loved and it was time to become *Me*. And in being me, I was done trying to make people understand. I'm going to be who I am whether you like it or not. You either get it or you don't. I'm ok with either.

Kayil York

It isn't asking for too much to require people to treat you right. It's an act of love for yourself. It's asking for common decency– which you undoubtedly deserve.

You can't have a healthy relationship with someone who is committed to having an unhealthy relationship with you. *Period.*

Kayil York

Even though it took me years to understood my worth, I won't forget what it cost me. I won't forget what it taught me. And I won't allow anyone to make me forget it either.

You've got to stop chasing people and trying to fix everything when you're the only one putting in the effort. I know the fixer in you is dying to put the pieces back together. But some people don't want the pieces to fall back into place. That's something you have to come to terms with in letting them go so you can find the peace you need to move on.

Kayil York

The important thing to know when it comes to communication, is that you're not just supposed to listen and reply. You need to understand what's being said and the emotions behind it. If you're listening to merely respond with a reaction but not listening to understand where they are coming from, you will have continuous unresolved miscommunication coupled with frustration.

Lacrimarium

Strong women are not born. They are built by their hardships. They are resilient because they refuse to stay down when they're knocked down. And above all they are humble in spirit because of the hell they get through no matter how difficult it is.

Kayil York

She put everyone's hearts above her own for too long. Because that's what she believed she needed to do. Until she realized the importance of putting her own heart first- because you can't take care of everyone else without first taking care of yourself.

Lacrimarium

It is never easy to have your heart bleed when someone hurts you. But as you weep, let those tears water your brokenness and allow yourself to bloom from it.

Kayil York

You have changed so much this year. It's ok to take time to pause and recognize that. Because you're not hurting from those things that broke you. You took the time to heal, you took the time to take a step back to work on yourself. You acknowledged the places you needed to work on and grew from that. You changed yourself and that should be celebrated. Because you've come such a long way and have so much to look forward to.

She wasn't aesthetically pleasing.
She liked to wear her own bright colors following her own trend. Standing out because she wasn't made to fit in.

Kayil York

One by one I let each tear
drip
drip
drip
into my vial of memories.
Maybe one day I'll look at
these tears and maybe it won't
hurt so much to remember the
reason I had to release them.

Healing feels a lot like dying when your pieces are crawling towards any kind of light that will help cease the pain. Healing will show you how strong you can be when you have no strength left to keep yourself from crying out to God that you're anything but fine.

Kayil York

Keep the souls that see the storms you go through and still choose to stick by you. Because when they allow the rain to get them wet without complaint, you know you have someone worth holding onto. Not everyone is willing to go through the hard times with you, so when those special ones do, don't let them go.

Lacrimarium

You have to be uncomfortable in order to grow. That means making your way through the dark in the dirt to get to the light. Blooming isn't just about the flower itself, it's about the journey and what it took to get yourself to make yourself bloom.

Kayil York

When you put yourself back together, you become indestructible. Don't be surprised when that scares other people away. Not everyone can share your bravery for picking up your own pieces because you refused to stay broken.

It's ok to be sympathetic towards other people's pain. Because we all get hurt, we all have our own problems we're working through and broken hearts we're trying to mend. What's not ok is constantly taking your pain out on other people that didn't cut you. While your pain is valid, try not to make others the collateral damage in your journey to healing. That's when you take time to yourself to focus on your wounds. Take the necessary space to clear your head so you can heal your heart.

Kayil York

If they are meant be in your life, you won't have to force anything. True connections are never forced, they just flow. If you lose someone, let it happen. Because the ending always allows a new beginning. There's so much give and take to life and you just have to try to appreciate what you have while you have it, and allow yourself to let go when its time to let go.

It's ok to become unavailable
to the people who show you
constant inconsistency.

Kayil York

Just like the responsibilities we have in our day to day lives; we must use that same practice when it comes to relationships. The access you give to others is a privilege and requires the kind of respect that will allow your relationships to deepen. When that access is violated, you have every right to establish secure boundaries to protect your heart.

Lacrimarium

The important thing to remember about healing your wounds is that you're not choosing to forget what happened. You are choosing to not allow it to hold you and control your life. It is the utmost powerful thing you can do to better yourself in achieving the most out of life.

Kayil York

After the pain had settled and I was able to catch my breath, I decided in that moment how to move forward. I was going to close myself off to the disrespect, even if it meant severing ties. I was going to set the necessary boundaries to protect my heart so people couldn't take advantage. I was going to forgive even though I didn't get an apology. Because I was not going to allow myself to be taken advantage of anymore. That means, I make no apologies for the collateral damage that causes.

Lacrimarium

I've reached this point in my life where I don't have time to fight with people who aren't trying to grow with me. If you want to work things through, let's do it. Don't waste my time if all you want to do is fight to be right.

Kayil York

It's ok to let people assume things about you, even if they're wrong. You can't please everyone, nor should you try. Just be yourself and the ones who don't belong will leave without the need to open your mouth.

I lost myself, I never fully came home. I just found a way to become a new version of myself so I wouldn't be someone going to war for the wrong person again.

Kayil York

You are going to work at it for a long time. Some days will be so grueling and difficult, and it'll feel like a non-stop cycle of trying and not seeing any results. Healing gets this way. Where you so desperately want to be better than the throbbing pain your brokenness makes you feel most the time. It isn't simple getting through. Because some days it takes everything in your soul not to be split to the bone. But remember in these days the importance of allowing your hurt to be transformed. You feel the pain so that when you heal, you appreciate the bloom that came from it.

Lacrimarium

People can't touch who you are now.
Because the changes you've incorporated into your life have made you evolve into someone entirely new. Even when they try to dig up who you used to be, it won't make a difference because you are not bound to where you have been the moment you knew you couldn't stay in a place that no longer holds the blood of who you used to be.

Kayil York

I used to think I wanted the words from people. The ones that feel good when you hear them. The ones that are full of promises and pure truths. But it wasn't until I grew up that I understood the value of the words are only as good as the actions that proceed them.

Lacrimarium

I let you go and haven't looked back. I forgave you for the apologies that were never given and the hurt you caused. And I made myself move on from you because my healing and peace of mind isn't going to be dependent on the way you think of me. Because I know I'm more valuable than the lack of human decency you treated me with.

Kayil York

It does make me sad when I think about the people I lost. We talk about letting people lose you, letting them go, and walking away with words like it's easy to do. But it takes a great deal of suffering, pain, and work to do that. Sometimes letting go looks a lot like pulling it right back to feel it one last time. To try and keep the good parts alive to kill the burn of the end.

Lacrimarium

Being in pain is hard.
But healing from it
will bring you the peace
you need to get to the other side.

Kayil York

Sometimes beginnings feel a lot like drowning. You suffocate until you're able to get your head above water, and then it all becomes clear. It is in the drowning, the suffocating, and the difficulty breathing, that we push through to get to where we didn't know we needed to be. Once you taste that air, that pure new air, it will prove to you the pain was worth getting through.

Forgive them anyway so you have peace in your soul. Heal yourself so that you're not passing down generational pain. Choose to move forward with your life so you're able to teach others how to do it when they don't feel like they can. Be the kind of person other people can take notes from because you weren't afraid of facing your fears, healing your pain, and living intentionally.

Kayil York

Detox your life.
Cut off the bad relationships
Heal your heart of the brokenness
Flush out your soul of any bitterness
Learn to get rid of things that aren't good
for you that build up inside that need to be
withdrawn from your life.

Lacrimarium

Life is difficult,
but you are strong enough
to live it well and with purpose.

Kayil York

Get rid of all the things that hold you back, don't help you grow, don't help you reach your goals or serve your purpose. Because those things have power in holding you down like an anchor. You have to let go of the burdens in order to receive the blessings.

There is a great importance in speaking things over your life. If you want something, whatever it may be, you need to call it forth. Because if you're speaking negatively about something you want before you've given it a chance to let it happen, then you're making sure it won't appear in your life. When you want something, declare that it will happen and then trust God to make it come to pass. Have a little faith and some patience- then watch your dreams unfold.

Kayil York

As you grow, you will stop dwelling on others close to you that aren't growing with you, lifting you up, and encouraging you.

You will hyperfocus on your rise and stop trying to help people get to where you are. Some people will not climb to the heights you will because not everyone has the courage you do to try.

Lacrimarium

Let your heart go out of bounds
for the ones you love.
Don't hold your heart in a cage
when love deserves to be set free.

Kayil York

You go through a great deal of pain trying to explain yourself without their ears hearing you. Trying to share your heart, laying bare your soul in the most vulnerable way to someone who merely takes advantage of what they can now use against you. There is great pain in being completely yourself and witnessing someone you love taking that and using it to satisfy their own selfish needs.

Lacrimarium

Every moment you spend not facing your pain–
Every moment you take shoving your problems down–
Every time you don't confront difficult situations–
Every time you push people away without resolving the issues between you–
Every time you choose chaos over peace... you slowly take your heart one more step away from healing–
You chip another piece of yourself out of place, taking away the life that was once within it.

Kayil York

Make sure the table you eat at
isn't filled with people waiting for you
to eat the food they poisoned.

No matter how you were raised, no matter who broke your heart, no matter what hand you were dealt. Only *YOU* have the power to unlearn what wasn't right. Only *YOU* can forgive the people who hurt you. And only *YOU* can decide how you want your life to turn out in spite of what they've done.

At the end of the day, recognize the responsibility you have in your hands and start living your life with the purpose of living it well.

Kayil York

Once you realize the power of saying no without an explanation and start applying it to your life, that is the start of standing up for yourself without apology. The beginning of trusting in who you are and not allowing anyone to keep you from being who you're called to be.

Lacrimarium

I stopped telling my side of the story and defending myself. Because I used to be the person that would talk myself to death with the truth, trying to reach an understanding or a resolution. But eventually I learned that certain people are just not for you and are only in your circle to talk about your circle. Now I don't explain myself., I let them talk. Because eventually they'll get the lies caught in their throat and choke.

Kayil York

No one talks about the brutality of healing. It starts by being broken, bruised, and bleeding. In order to start the healing process, you've got to scrape out anything that can cause infection. You've got to feel the pain of touching a wound you never wanted in the first place. You've got to burn, to taste the agony in order to feel the healing start. It is brutal, it is ugly, and it damn well hurts.

Lacrimarium

When you grow up and understand what it means to stand up for yourself, to speak out about what you want and what you need- make sure you apologize to yourself for all the times you didn't before you understood how to.

Kayil York

There's an importance in talking things out, in explaining your feelings, and telling others what's going on inside you. Because doing the opposite sure as hell doesn't get you anywhere and can't keep being the norm for today. It will undo and crumble relationships that should be lasting.

Speak your heart, speak your mind, and know it solves more problems than keeping your mouth shut will.

Lacrimarium

In my experience, people will hold onto the memory of you they had when they held the most control over you. That's why they get upset when you change. Because now you know how to stand up for yourself and don't allow them to walk all over you anymore.

Kayil York

The older I get, the more peace I value.
Which means not putting up with things
or people that disrupt it.

Lacrimarium

When you get out of that toxic relationship, make sure you don't just leave. But that you find and heal that place inside of you that attracted them to you in the first place. Otherwise, you will meet them again, at a different time with a different face.

Kayil York

Closure looks a lot like heartbreak but feels more like understanding what you have to let go of, and being ok with letting it go.

Lacrimarium

The trick is
to heal yourself
so that you don't
become like the
people who hurt you.

Kayil York

God only aligns things in your life that are for you. The simplest way to tell is that those things will bring clarity to a clouded mind and peace to a troubled heart.

Lacrimarium

You're better off without them.
The people who wronged you, hurt you, threw you under the bus and didn't bat an eye.
Let those people walk away. Because letting those people go is the catalyst for your growth.

Kayil York

When you don't allow people to walk all over you anymore, the narrative will change. You'll become the villain in their story because you won't be giving them what they have had no problem taking from you. But at least in your story, you'll be free.

Make sure that the value people place on you is based on who you are as a person, not on how much you can give to them.

Kayil York

Sometimes you have to stop being the only one that puts the effort in the relationship. There comes a point where you need to step back and let the ship go down. You gave more than you should have to a one-sided relationship and now it's time to let go.

Lacrimarium

My heart is full of memories.
Memories that strike your soul.
Memories that haunt your dreams.
Memories that keep the pain at bay.
The kind of Memories that just hurt deeply.
Memories full of you.

Kayil York

I let you go and haven't looked back.
I forgave you for the apologies that were never given and the hurt you caused. And I made myself move on from you because my healing and peace of mind isn't going to be dependent on the way you think of me. Because I know I'm more valuable than the lack of human decency you treated me with.

People who constantly disrupt your peace are not worth being in your life. If you constantly feel uneasy being around certain people, there's a reason for it. Listen to your gut and let those people go.

Kayil York

One of the hardest roads to walk down is forgiving yourself for your past mistakes. You loved too hard and lost too much and that made it difficult to accept that it broke your heart because of the decisions you made. But that's how we learn, by acknowledging what happened, how we got there, and learning what to look out for in the future.

Lacrimarium

This storm is your transition.
Ride with it. Hurt in it.
It's taking you away from this place
so you can show up where
you deserve to be at.

Kayil York

I used to have the worst anxiety that weighed on me from mistakes that I made. Giving my heart away to the wrong person ate at me like vultures pecking the flesh from my bones. I could feel the pull of each piece being stripped from me. As if they were never meant to be tied to me at all. As if the years I spent cracking my heart open never meant anything when the goodbye of silence replaced the hand that held me differently than anyone else had. The gripping disappointment of not being wanted makes you feel like a discarded rag thrown in the corner of forgotten. Shoving those feelings down, I would sit and drown myself in the beauty of numbness. Trying to just avoid the bleeding and thinking that maybe if I just don't look it will stop. The pain would take itself away and by the time I would turn to look, I wouldn't have anything to deal with but the memories. But grief speaks in different ways and each stage is hard to grasp because of each layer it pulls back to expose. I'm trying to get better at healing places that hurt more than I'd like. I've got to remember it's a process. Because you can't build something whole in a day. But I damn well will pick up a brick– one at a time and do my best to get there. No matter how long it takes. I will rebuild what was broken.

You shouldn't have to explain why you deserve to be spoken to with respect and treated with human decency. Do not allow anyone, even if it's someone you love, to talk down to you, hurt you, or strip you of who you are in order to gain power over you. That isn't love. And it sure as hell isn't how you should ever be treated.

Kayil York

Some people have the capability to strip you of who you are. They can make you fear making your own decisions because you just know they won't like it or accept the outcome. All because of love. Which is why it makes it so powerful. The connection of souls. So be sure your connections breathe life into you. Not smother you.

If you're in that dark place, stuck in the circle of black swallowing your hope… I'm telling you it's ok to be there. We have to know the darkness to a certain degree in order to know how to reach for the light. No journey is ever without the grounds of gritting your teeth, fighting your demons, and not allowing them to take the blood from your veins. We have to know the darkness to appreciate the light.

Kayil York

Grief shows the depth
of love we had for what
becomes lost out of our control.

If you ask me who I am, I will tell you of all the ways I have transformed out of and into. I am constantly becoming, renewing. without apology, without regret.

Kayil York

You've healed too much to not raise your standards on who you have relationships with and who you allow to have access to you.

Lacrimarium

When it comes to the potential of long-term things, be sure you're not throwing it away because the stress of what's happening in that moment is difficult.

Kayil York

You're hurting this badly because you loved them deeply. They meant something to you. Built a home within you only to leave you. It hurts this much because you gave it all hope, nourished its potential, and didn't see how the crumbling of dreams can leave such a painful scar.

Forgive them for the pain, even though you would have never hurt them the same way. You may not have deserved the pain, but you deserve the healing that comes with forgiving them.

Lacrimarium

You don't need to have the last word. It took me a long time to understand that. But once you've said your peace, you have no reason to keep justifying what they refuse to understand.

Kayil York

The tears you shed for them don't go unnoticed. Every single cry you've pierced the sky with, begging with God to take the pain away, all has meaning. The nights you spent soaking your pillow with screams of disappointment and confusion on how to get through what you're going through, are not for nothing. God sees your tears, honors them, and holds them. *They will all be redeemed in time.*

Lacrimarium

There will be many people you will cross paths with. Not all of them will understand your flame and the way you burn. What I have learned the hard way is that you shouldn't dim your spark to keep them from burning. If they can't handle you, either let them go or keep burning and eventually they'll go away.

Kayil York

Your spirit will feel disrupted when you're not around the right people. Listen to that intuition. That voice is there to recognize what your eyes may not be able to spot. Learn how to pay attention when it's telling you something is off. It's usually right.

Forgive them anyway. Cry out the pain of having to let them go. Forgive them again, even when it becomes too much to handle.

Soon, healing will come.

Oceans are being released in your heart and crashing into your soul. When it comes to that kind of storm, give yourself some time to heal. Forgiveness sometimes is a repeated act that has to be practiced again and again because the pain was so great and so heavy. You start to take a layer off one at a time.

Hurt, bleed, heal.
Hurt, bleed, heal.
Hurt, bleed, heal.

You keep going, you forgive again. Until the pain is gone and the raging oceans are now calm. Still waters will finally bring peace to the chaos.

Kayil York

I make every effort to work things out. I will fight and plead and give everything I have to work through the difficult times.
But when I have nothing left to say, nothing left to give, you will know I'm done. I have learned you can only do so much to fix certain situations. Some people just don't want to work it out with you. Once you understand that, it will get easier to cut ties so you're not stuck dealing with a relationship that has no future.

Lacrimarium

You don't need to prove your point.
You don't have to explain yourself.
You don't have to try and force them to see what
they refuse to acknowledge.

Remove yourself from the equation,
Because healing and peace reside
in the places that don't require you
to belittle yourself for the sake
of keeping company with the ones
only out to hurt you.

Kayil York

As hard as it may be,
you have to let go of the pain
and all of the baggage that
comes along with it.

The only thing you should
be taking into your future
are the lessons learned
from what's being
left behind.

One of the safest ways we feel loved
is by being who we've always wanted to be,
and we aren't being told–
"you're not enough"
"you could be better"
"be less" –

You are able to truly be yourself, without the need
to have to explain why you are the way you are.

Kayil York

The more you grow and learn, the less you will put up with. Because the levels you are reaching won't allow access to people who aren't aligning with your purpose.

Lacrimarium

After all these years, I don't want certain people in my life, in my business, or a part of my journey.
Because I know what it means to sacrifice who you are for people who wouldn't bother lifting a finger for you.

Kayil York

There have been times I would take pieces of myself away to try and gain acceptance from others. I would hide myself because the fear of not being wanted was scarier than being alone.

It wasn't until there were no pieces left of me to give that I realized how much time I wasted trying to gain what was never valuable in the first place.

Now I boldly stand out in who I am.
I make no apologies for being someone
you can't be around.
I know better now.

The most valuable lessons you can learn are the ones when you allow yourself permission to let go of people who don't give a second thought to losing you.
Let them go.
Walk away and distance yourself.
You can't always be the one trying to save what's already been undone.

Kayil York

I don't accept disrespect anymore.
I spent too much of my life being forced to swallow words and actions that I was not ok with.
Taking away my voice little by little.
Not anymore.
Disrespect equals detachment.

Healing myself is rough.
Because after all the pieces are put back together, replaced, or renewed, you are not the same person you were before.

You're entirely new.
Take the time to learn who you are now.

Give yourself the necessary grace to figure out where you're meant to go from here.

Kayil York

If you want toxic people
to stop choking the life
from you–
you've got to stop giving
them the rope to do it.

–cut the ties

Lacrimarium

Please don't paint their red flags green because you love them. Because eventually the paint will wear and the mask you tried to cover them with will show you what was there all along.

Kayil York

You have to let go of people that have shown you time and time again they don't value you, so you can truly see your worth.

Lacrimarium

The more peace you
want in your life,
the more people
you'll be ok with
letting go
to achieve it.

Kayil York

There comes a point where you have to stop running from your feelings. You have to stop and claim them. Recognize where it hurts, where your soul is disturbed. There's only so long you can go without acknowledging your feelings before the numbness starts to root and grow in places it should not be.

Not everyone is going to understand your heart.
They may not like what they see either, but that's because they don't understand what it took to mold it. They don't understand the journey and the pain you've endured to become this soft. Nobody knows the violence it took to get this kind of peace in accepting who you are. Don't allow their skewed perception of you to invalidate the progress you made in accepting and loving who you've become.

Kayil York

There are days when I don't feel like I'm good enough. When I feel as if all I've worked so hard for is going downhill and I don't know how to get back to where I was.

Sometimes when we feel at our lowest and are about to give up, that's when the biggest breakthrough is about to happen. *This is the part where you don't give up. This is the part where you push through.*

This part of her life has taken the biggest piece from her. It has shaken her, stripped her, and has worn her down to the bone. But even though this part is difficult, she still strapped on her bravery and laced her spine with courage to face what she knows she can conquer.

Kayil York

If you want people to respect your boundaries, then you have to be serious when it comes to setting them.

That means not allowing their violation of those boundaries to be minimized because of the fear of confronting what they disrespected.

Don't be afraid to go into ghost mode
when it comes to bettering yourself.
Dive deep into healing your heart.
Fix the parts of yourself that are toxic.
Keep your focus.
Restore peace inside your soul.
Sometimes the best strategy in having
a peaceful life is moving in silence
where no one can try and control
your progression.

Kayil York

If I go quiet, it's because it was time to let you know where I stood. I'm done being the one always coming through for you and you never coming through for me. I'm done constantly reaching out to clear silence bouncing off the backend, with no cares given. I won't hold it against you. But I've got to do what's best for me, and that's by moving forward without you.

You know you've changed when you stop being there for every single person who was never there for you. You know you've changed when you start putting yourself first. Sometimes it takes going through a great deal of pain to make you understand why change is necessary to protect your heart.

Kayil York

When someone is constantly mistreating you despite your efforts to make peace. It's time to let them go. Better to remove their access to you than put up with constant disrespect.

Forgive them on purpose—
plant peace in your soul.
Heal yourself so that you're
not passing down generational pain.
Choose to move forward with
your life so you're able to teach
others how to do it when they
don't feel like they can.

Be the kind of person people can take notes from because you weren't afraid of facing your fears, healing your pain, and living intentionally.

Kayil York

When the most intense part of life feels like it's cutting your legs from under you, that's when you have to be brave enough to push through your fear to give up. I know the weight that kind of fear holds on your heart. How gripping its hand can keep your throat tight with anxiety. How the thought of being able to make it through what just destroyed you, seems impossible. But all it takes is a small piece of faith to move. And with each move, each small step, it will build more confidence within yourself to keep going. All it takes is just that small bit of faith, that's where it starts.

The truth is– you can't prevent the hurt that comes with living in this world. But you can heal from it. We will be met with great tragedy, sorrow, and pain. Met with unrelenting agony from the different ways our hearts shatter by the people we gave ourselves to. We can't prevent the damage from happening to us, but we have all the power in restoring the brokenness. It may take some time, but from every piece of ash you will bloom into something more. Someone better than before. Someone stronger with a little more experience and wisdom to take you through the next seasons.

Kayil York

The end of our pain rouses the spirit of change. Being at a place that has held your feet to the bottom of hells door can rile up the right amount of courage to cut the rope to set yourself free into the arms of healing.

One of the hardest things in life is having to change your mindset to understand the way life really is and not how you hope it's going to be. When you're the one who trusts too easily because you have so much hope in other people, and that trust gets destroyed time and time again. You have to stop, heal yourself from not having the right wisdom, and set the necessary boundaries to protect yourself from people who don't have your best interests at heart from here on out.

Kayil York

Some people are good at misunderstanding who you are. So let them. You shouldn't have to keep fighting for someone to hear you when they choose to ignore you. You shouldn't' have to beg and plead for them to stay when they want to leave. That is something I've had to face and understand that has taken me most of my life to get through my head.

For years I would fight and plead and beg for people to stay. To work on things. To pick a part everything to find where we went wrong. Trying to put back together a puzzle that keeps coming unpieced. Trying to calm the chaos, put out the fire, and fix the situation. I bent over backwards until it broke me. I burn until I burn out. I fight until I'm bloody and exhausted with defeat. Sinking for us, alone. I am too much for myself a lot of the time, not knowing how to go about anything because my mind is racing in every direction and I'm not sure what road to follow. But I know that with every step I take, it's going to lead me in the right direction. I just have to trust myself to trust that God won't bring me to a place I'm not meant to be in.

Lacrimarium

I'm learning to step back. Learning to take a little more time to myself and not give so much that I'm below empty. I'm learning to breathe better, learning how to calm the aching in my mind before it spreads through my body. I'm breaking down the fears that like to ride inside my backbone. I'm healing more for myself than I ever have. To be more. To be better. It took some major shifting to refocus. But it got me in a place I won't compromise for anyone.

It's difficult not to allow the opinions of others to break you down, even though you know who you are down to your core. When you're confident to walk forward without looking side to side, you know you've hit a victory where you don't feel the need to compromise yourself at the expense of pleasing the ones around you.

When you reach this place, walk with the confidence it deserves. Because the journey it took you through is not for the faint of heart.

Kayil York

Authenticity is revealed by actions.
You show who you are by what you do.

Lacrimarium

Look out for the ones who are quick to correct, yet do nothing when their own wrong doings are being questioned. No relationship is safe when they can't take accountability for their own mistakes.

Kayil York

There are versions of me I have left behind. I had to let them go when they stopped being relevant to where my growth was going.

Lacrimarium

Trust me, you are far too loved to think
the world would be better off without you.
It's a rough patch, not a permanent hell.

You deserve to be here.

Whatever your mind is trying to trick you into believing, I will help you. Come sit with me and I'll help you see your strength so you can make it through this.

Kayil York

No matter how hurt and broken you may feel, you are an incredibly strong and courageous person. Even when the people you relied on the most have let you down, you still wake up every day to face the world. Making sure that every step you take is filled with courage and without fear.

Lacrimarium

You don't owe anyone
an apology for healing yourself
beyond their recognition of what's
acceptable.

Kayil York

The most mature thing you can do to better yourself is recognizing the parts of yourself that are broken and healing them. Recognizing where you are toxic and changing your patterns. And practicing taking care of yourself so that you're not treating others wrongly based on the filter of your wounds.

Lacrimarium

Once you stop being afraid of what they think, it becomes easier to let them judge you.
I say let them.
Nothing is braver than standing up and out in who you are. Because no one knows the fire you went through and the changes you endured to become this unphased.

Kayil York

I hope you find the strength within you to leave when they cause nothing but confusion and dishonesty. It may not be the easiest thing to do, but at least you'll understand that you deserve more than someone who only gives as little as possible in order to take the maximum from you.

Lacrimarium

Most of life is figuring out what you want by knowing what you don't want. Failed relationships always teach us something we may not realize, even if we believe it should have been more than what it turned out to be. The best things in life come after the greatest failures of our life.

Kayil York

When I put myself back together again, I left out the pieces of you because you didn't belong there anymore. I put myself back together to be different on purpose so I know what healing looks like without the pain of your broken pieces clouding my memory.

Lacrimarium

It's ok if you stayed longer than you should. Sometimes it takes us a while to take off the rose-colored glasses they kept forcing you to wear. But once you see through to who they are, walking away will help you recognize what to look out for the next time love comes calling.

Kayil York

I see the pain in your eyes and the wars you don't speak of. I see how difficult it is to voice your pain, you wear it the way the sky cracks when it's ready to break down in rain. I see your scars; I may not know how each one took its place without you asking or wanting them. I see you in all your brokenness and still see you as worthy.
Entirely worthy.

Lacrimarium

If you want to change,
you have to be comfortably uncomfortable
with confronting the toxic parts
of yourself and being brave enough
to cut them out of you.

Kayil York

Anyone who disrespects, belittles, betrays, mistreats, abuses, and hurts you *consistently… Deserves nothing but distance from you.*

Walk away from people who don't value you.
Walk away from people who mistreat you.
Walk away from situations you know you're not supposed to be in.
Walk away from people who don't reciprocate the same effort.
Walk away from what isn't right for you so you can accept the lessons and continue your journey in walking the path God has laid out for you.

Kayil York

If they're uncomfortable with your boundaries, they may be one of the reasons you needed to create them.
Let them be bothered.
At least you'll be at peace.

Lacrimarium

The dirt you threw on me to try and intimidate, showed me how to grow in the most troubling situations. Instead of being buried, I grew into a stronger, better version of who you couldn't keep under the dirt.

Kayil York

I wish you the best.
Even though you were not meant
to be in my life, doesn't mean
I don't want you to have what's
best in yours.

Lacrimarium

If you have to give up who you are to get what you want. Whether it's a job, relationship, or circumstance- *don't do it.*
Because losing yourself is not an easy road to come back from. And chances are, there is something better out there that you won't have to compromise yourself to get. You may just have to have a little patience to get it.

Kayil York

You're allowed to miss people you had to let go of. It's never easy to move on without the ones you thought would be with you for the long haul.

There are people I miss very dearly. Doesn't mean I would change where I am or go back and change what's already done. But there are days when their memory is heavy on my mind and I can't help but ache in all the places they left their mark on.

Lacrimarium

Have you ever ached so much you feel your heart misplace itself to find what is no longer there? There is a missing piece you grasp for that left you long ago. A painful twinge when the season changes without you. A seemingly unbearable reality that the parts of you that you thought were whole are actually a quiet wound that just hasn't had the light hit it enough to hurt.

Kayil York

And when the hard days hit, try to remind yourself that it will still be alright even if you're not feeling alright. The waves have to hit the shore from time to time before the horizon can get its peace back.

Lacrimarium

Everything that has shaped me,
I have learned to appreciate.

The pain of a broken heart
Failed relationships
The broken roads
The cliffs I had to walk off of
The anxiety of the unknown

I have learned the value
of every failed part of my life
was so that I could walk into
the biggest blessings of my life.

Kayil York

Not everyone is capable of handling what you're able to give them. It isn't because they don't want it. But some people were not raised with knowing what real love and care is. Some have been burned too much that when it comes to seeing something real, it only triggers them to run.

The amazing thing about music- it may not answer your questions but it hears you. Listens to you. Aches with you. Hurts with you. Empathizes with every feeling and emotion you have and gives you a sense of being heard. Music is my lifeblood.
The poetry of another realm, always there to meet us where we are.

Kayil York

If walking away is the last step you had to take, be at peace knowing it wasn't from lack of trying to take every other step possible from having to walk away.

When people truly care about you, they will show it. It doesn't have to be all the time because life is crazy and we all get busy. But there will be a consistency in showing you you're loved so you never have to think to question it.

Kayil York

Life is too short to be surrounded by negativity. It's important to walk away from people who aren't helping serve your purpose, supporting your dreams, and cheering you on.

Prioritize your happiness by surrounding yourself with people who truly believe in you.

Lacrimarium

Don't let anyone dim your light or put out your flames. Instead, use their lack of understanding as motivation to push forward and prove them wrong. Believe in yourself and your abilities, and don't let anyone else's opinions or actions hold you back from achieving your dreams. Remember, your fire is unique to you, and it's up to you to keep it burning strong.

Kayil York

It's better to spend some time alone so you can truly work on bettering yourself without the noise of everyone else telling you what you should or shouldn't be doing.

You can go quiet and let them assume the worst. Because sometimes you have to heal in silence. That means letting people assume what they will without allowing it to hurt your progression.

Kayil York

When someone has caused you emotional pain, it's crucial not to retaliate in anger.
Shift your focus to forgiving them and then walking away to work towards healing yourself.

Lacrimarium

The moment you start questioning how much abuse you can endure, should be the moment that tells you this isn't right. No relationship should make you question how much you can take, because love was never meant to be tolerant of that kind of pain that strips you of your identity.

Kayil York

I care less now. In the sense that for some people I don't care more for. You are no longer a priority in my life for a reason. Whether we had a falling out, or it was time to go our separate ways. I still care for you, but it no longer holds my attention like it used to. I will still love you, still want the best for you, and still wish you all the happiness in the world. Just from a distance.

Lacrimarium

I won't tell you what to do because I've been there and I understand how difficult it is. But if there's one piece of advice I could give you, it's that you don't want to waste your time loving someone alone. It is a painful road that is hard to recover from. There is no way for you to make it what it should be, because the other person should be contributing more than what you think is acceptable.

Kayil York

I have a substantial amount of motivation to make sure my life is anything but ordinary.
That is the way I live.
With intent, without fear.

Lacrimarium

People change you.
Some come into your life
and dig a hole in your heart.
Others build graves in your soul.
Even when that person leaves your life,
doesn't mean they've fully left.
Depending on how many fingerprints they imprinted will only show you how much your soul eclipsed with their own.

Kayil York

The world did not love her for who she was.
But that was the point.
You don't need to be liked
in order to be who you are.

Lacrimarium

It took me a while, but I stopped trying to be in places with people I was not meant to be with. Once I realized and understood who I was, I found how important it is to surround yourself with people who are like minded. Even if you're alone, at least you're not being held back.

Kayil York

Don't mistake my kindness
for unstable boundaries.

Where my walls stand
are a sign of how much
I've learned from lacking them.

I am kind, but I will not
allow you to disrespect
my house. If you do,
I'll show you the door.

Lacrimarium

Make sure you don't shrink yourself to the size that other people can stand because you're afraid of embracing your value.

Kayil York

Forgive–
even though you may
never get an apology.

Because healing is your
responsibility and it's up to you
to restore your peace.

I think you're brave because you chose to let go of what held the most control over you.

Because doing that isn't easy and can take away a huge part of you. But the beauty of letting go is being able to rebuild yourself without their hands telling you how high you can go.

Kayil York

I'll pray for you.

I'm not the kind to wish anything wrong to happen to you. But when the door has come to a close, I wish you the best as far away from me as possible.

Lacrimarium

It's exhausting, isn't it?
Holding on to all of that anger…

I promise you'll find your breath as soon as you lay it all down and let it go.

Kayil York

You have to put them back in the past. You can't keep bringing them into your *now,* because they are stealing away the moments that they are no longer a part of. Keep them in the past, where they belong. Out of your heart, into the memory.

Lacrimarium

Sometimes you're uncomfortable in the place you're in because it's time to move out of it into a new place.

Kayil York

Peace comes with distance when it comes to certain people. Sometimes taking time away is the exact thing you need in order to see how people affect you. When they cause more disruption to your spirit than they do peace, you know that connection isn't right for you.

Lacrimarium

Having gone through the trauma of loss can put you on high alert at all terms. It keeps your body at an all-time high of trying to stay safe when you've felt like there's danger at every turn. Because people are not as they seem and it can become entirely exhausting trying to gain relationships that ultimately kill your desire to want anyone around you.

Kayil York

There will be people who would rather lose you so they don't have to change their unhealthy patterns in order to have a healthy relationship with you.

It's ok to let them go.

You have to balance out your life. Yes, it's important to be positive and have a good mindset that helps your drive in achieving your goals. But you also have to honor the pain that comes with that. The losses pile up and weigh heavy on our heart and ignoring it with the face of happiness will not help your progression. The balance comes with knowing how to allow pain to be just as present as happiness. You can't have one without the other.

Kayil York

As an adult you see how you were able to hide your trauma growing up. Because the fear of disappointing or not being accepted outweighed knowing your own personality. In turn, stealing years of being yourself in the name of obedience.

I hope that when you find who you are, you don't allow anyone to ever dictate how you should be because their view of you is not how you see yourself.

Lacrimarium

With all the pain you caused, you have left me no choice but to move on. I barely made it out with what little was left of me. I have to do what's best for me now. And as hard as it is, that means leaving you out of who I plan on becoming once I've healed.

Kayil York

Fighting through the fear is the hardest part. But once you get to the other side, you realize just how much strength you have inside you when you're forced to get through the pain alone.

One of the hardest parts of life is having to sit with your pain alone because no one tries to sit with you to understand it.

Kayil York

At the end of the day, I hope you choose healing. There are is far too much bitterness in this world that holds us captive in places we are never meant to be in for long. I hope that you choose to heal your heart and forgive the people that broke you. It can be hard to let that pain go because of how deep their hold twisted and shook you. But you deserve peace. You deserve a new story that doesn't allow their hold to control you anymore.

I pray that wherever you're at in your life right now that you choose to let go of everything that's hindering, holding, controlling, and manipulating you and I hope you can let it go.

LET IT GO.
Let it go.

Let go and heal yourself.

Lacrimarium

Some of us have wars we never quite come home from and pains we don't talk about. But then there are some wars we have to talk about in order to heal what should have never happened to us.

Kayil York

After we have been shattered, we must put those broken pieces into the ink of our pens, the paint in our bristles, and into pools on our paper. We must let the chaos be *seen, felt, and honored* for the changes they've made within us and the lessons they have taught us.

Lacrimarium

Kayil York

I hope and pray that everything you want in this life be met. That every tear will be redeemed for the heartache it brought. That every piece of your heart that's broken will be restored.
I pray for your renewal.
That peace will meet you where it needs to and whatever is holding you back from it will break its hold from you.

With all my love,
Kayil

Lacrimarium

Kayil York

*Whatever is weighing on your heart, I encourage you to write it down here in this blank space. Once you do, rip this page out, and burn it.
As a way of letting go of the hard things.*

Say it all here:

Made in United States
North Haven, CT
28 January 2024

48038131R00117